MOVERS, SHAKERS, & HISTORY MAKERS

NIKOLA TESLA

ENGINEER WITH ELECTRIC IDEAS

CONTENT CONSULTANT
ERIK STAUFFER
PhD, ELECTRICAL ENGINEERING

BY EMILY HUDD

CAPSTONE PRESS
a capstone imprint

Capstone Captivate is published by Capstone Press, an imprint of Capstone.
1710 Roe Crest Drive
North Mankato, Minnesota 56003
www.capstonepub.com

Library of Congress Cataloging-in-Publication Data
Names: Hudd, Emily, author.
Title: Nikola Tesla : engineer with electric ideas / by Emily Hudd.
Description: North Mankato, Minnesota : Capstone Press, [2021] | Series:
  Movers, shakers, and history makers | Includes index. | Audience: Grades
  4-6
Identifiers: LCCN 2020000925 (print) | LCCN 2020000926 (ebook) | ISBN
  9781496684790 (hardcover) | ISBN 9781496688217 (paperback) | ISBN
  9781496684998 (pdf)
Subjects: LCSH: Tesla, Nikola, 1856-1943—Juvenile literature. | Electrical
  engineers—United States—Biography—Juvenile literature. |
  Scientists—United States—Biography—Juvenile literature. |
  Inventors—United States—Biography—Juvenile literature.
Classification: LCC TK140.T4 H78 2020 (print) | LCC TK140.T4 (ebook) |
  DDC 621.3092 [B]—dc23
LC record available at https://lccn.loc.gov/2020000925
LC ebook record available at https://lccn.loc.gov/2020000926

Image Credits
Alamy: North Wind Picture Archives, 13, Science History Images, 32; iStockphoto: ZU_09, 21; Library of Congress: Bain News Service, cover (foreground), H.C. White Co., 16, Joseph G. Gessford, 26; Newscom: akg-images, 10, Album/Fine Art Images, 5, Everett Collection, 42; Science Source: 25, New York Public Library, 35, 36, Photo Researchers, 19; Shutterstock Images: Aliona Manakova, 14 (light bulb), Ase, cover (background), 1, e2dan, 30, Everett Historical, 29, Kanate, 38, MarySan, 14 (battery), Oleksiy Mark, 9, xbrchx, 7

Editorial Credits
Editor: Marie Pearson; Designer: Colleen McLaren; Production Specialist: Ryan Gale

All internet sites appearing in back matter were available and accurate when this book was sent to press.

Printed in the United States of America.
PA117

CONTENTS

CHAPTER ONE

MEASURING IN TESLAS............................4

CHAPTER TWO

THE START OF A RIVALRY........................12

CHAPTER THREE

STRUGGLING TO MAKE IT
ON HIS OWN.......................................18

CHAPTER FOUR

PARTNERSHIPS AND INVENTIONS............24

CHAPTER FIVE

ECCENTRIC MAN, LASTING LEGACY.........34

TIMELINE..44
GLOSSARY...46
READ MORE/INTERNET SITES................................47
INDEX...48

Words in **bold** are in the glossary.

CHAPTER ONE

MEASURING IN TESLAS

Few people have a unit of measurement named after them. But Nikola Tesla does! Tesla was an inventor in the late 1800s and early 1900s. He made many discoveries in the field of electricity. In 1960, the General Conference on Weights and Measures honored him. It named the unit that measures magnetic field strength the *tesla*. A magnetic field pulls metals such as steel toward it. Teslas are often used to measure extremely large and powerful magnetic fields. One example is a magnetic resonance imaging (MRI) machine. This machine uses magnets to take detailed images of people's bodies.

The tesla was given its name 17 years after the inventor's death. Today, Tesla is remembered as a genius and one of history's groundbreaking inventors.

Today, Nikola Tesla is known as a brilliant inventor. He made many contributions to science.

Tesla didn't get many awards or much recognition for his ideas when he was alive. During his lifetime, he wasn't always successful. But Tesla worked hard to make sure his scientific discoveries could help people.

EARLY LIFE OF NIKOLA TESLA

Nikola was born July 10, 1856, in Smiljan, Croatia. His father was a priest. His mother ran the family farm. His older brother, Dane, was killed in a riding accident when Nikola was 5 years old. The painful memory stayed with Nikola throughout his life.

NIKOLA TESLA MUSEUM

The Nikola Tesla Museum is in Belgrade, Serbia. It lets people explore Tesla's ideas and inventions. People can even take **virtual reality** tours. They strap a device onto their head. It covers their eyes, and they watch a screen. During the tour, people experience a virtual environment. They see an image of Tesla, who explains his inventions and ideas. The tour shows viewers important locations from his life, such as his home and his laboratory in Colorado.

People can visit the Nikola Tesla Memorial Center in Smiljan. It includes Tesla's restored childhood home.

Nikola was a bright student. He realized his passion for science as a teen. But his father wanted him to be a priest. Nikola became dangerously ill with cholera when he was 17. For a year, he battled the illness and could do little else. During this time, his father softened. He just wanted Nikola to survive. He agreed with Nikola's wishes to study science if he got healthy. After Nikola recovered, he continued his education.

FACT

Tesla's mother didn't go to school. But she had a great memory and showed a natural skill with machines.

TESLA'S PARENTS

Tesla said he got his creativity from his mother. She invented a mechanical eggbeater and other machines to help with daily farm life. Tesla's father wrote poetry. Tesla also read and wrote poetry. Sometimes he would recite poems.

Nikola went to the Polytechnic Institute in Graz, in what is now Austria. He worked hard and quickly became a top student. One day he got into an argument with a professor. The professor was teaching about direct current (DC) motors. DC is a type of electricity. It works by having electricity flow in only one direction. It was the only option for electricity at the time.

Nikola thought there were flaws in the DC motor design. The professor disagreed. Nikola soon dropped out of school. But he took an idea with him. Nikola thought a different type of motor, powered by alternating current (AC), could work better than a DC motor. AC works by quickly changing the direction electricity flows.

Today, Prague is the capital of the Czech Republic. Many universities are located in Prague.

There was just one problem. Nikola didn't know how to make an AC motor work. The leaders in electricity at the time focused on DC power.

Nikola started attending the University of Prague in what is now the Czech Republic to finish his education. While there, he became addicted to gambling. He lost all his money. He quit school to find a job. But he never stopped thinking about the AC motor.

Women were often hired to send and receive telegraphs.

FAMOUS IDEA

By 1882, Tesla was working at a telegraph office in Budapest, Hungary. One day he suddenly got an idea for an AC motor. He sketched it in the sand during a walk. The idea was for a rotating magnetic field. It used spinning magnetic fields to power a machine.

Tesla could picture the whole AC motor in his head. He tried to imagine how it could be used. Eventually, he realized this idea could change the way motors and electric systems worked. Rotating magnetic fields would become part of Tesla's famous invention, the AC motor.

CHAPTER TWO

THE START OF A RIVALRY

Tesla's idea for alternating current power was a major discovery. But it wasn't popular right away. Direct current power was widely used.

Tesla moved to Paris, France, in 1882 for a job repairing DC power plants. Power plants are factories that make electricity for nearby cities. At that job, Tesla worked for the Continental Edison Company. The company belonged to Thomas Edison.

Edison was a famous American inventor. He had invented a way to bring electricity into people's homes. The system used DC power. Towers, cables, and wires connected the electricity to buildings. People could turn on lights with the flip of a switch.

Some streets in New York were lit with electric streetlights in the 1880s.

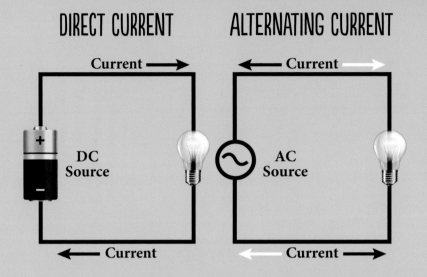

DIRECT CURRENT

ALTERNATING CURRENT

AC power works by quickly changing the direction electricity flows. First it flows in the direction of the white arrow. Then it reverses, flowing in the direction of the black arrow. DC works by sending electricity in one direction. It is less efficient at distributing power over long distances than AC.

In 1882, Manhattan in New York City became one of the first places where some people had in-home electricity. The spread of electricity happened slowly. But Edison saw great potential for his invention.

MOVING OVERSEAS

Tesla was a talented electrical **engineer**. He worked in Paris for a few years. During that time, he was noticed by Charles Batchelor, one of Edison's trusted leaders at the power plant. Batchelor sent a letter to Edison in New York telling him that Tesla was very smart. Soon after, Edison invited Tesla to work for him in the United States. In 1884, Tesla set sail with few belongings. He had four cents and some papers folded in his pockets. The papers had poems and invention ideas scribbled on them.

Tesla took a job as an engineer at Edison's headquarters in New York City. Both men were brilliant inventors. They both worked in electrical engineering. But they didn't always get along.

FACT

In the late 1920s, Tesla wrote a poem titled "Fragments of Olympian Gossip." The poem makes fun of scientists, including Isaac Newton and Albert Einstein.

Thomas Edison was making DC electricity generators in the 1880s. These generators could power lamps and other electric devices.

Edison supported DC power. He had put a lot of money and work into its development. Tesla believed AC power was the future of electricity. It was more efficient and able to deliver more power.

THE TRICKY DEAL

In 1884, Edison offered Tesla a deal. He asked Tesla to improve the design of DC dynamos. Dynamos are machines that turn energy into electricity. They're also known as generators. When wires in the machine spin, they generate electricity. Then the electricity can be sent out and used.

If Tesla succeeded, Edison said he would give Tesla $50,000. That sum is equal to more than $1.4 million in today's dollars. Tesla experimented for months. He gave Edison a better design and asked for the money. But Edison never paid Tesla. Tesla was bitter about that. He quit working for Edison soon after. Tesla focused on improving AC power on his own.

CHAPTER THREE

STRUGGLING TO MAKE IT ON HIS OWN

Tesla struggled to find work after leaving the job with Edison. Around 1885, he started his own company. But he couldn't get enough financial support to create a full AC system. He tried to explain how it would be successful. But people didn't believe his alternating current idea would work. Or they didn't think it would be more successful than Edison's business. For a time in 1886, Tesla had to dig ditches for power lines and telephone poles. To make matters worse, the company he dug for belonged to Edison.

Tesla was not a skilled businessman. He didn't turn his inventions into money-making products as many others did. He preferred to focus his time on inventing.

Tesla wasn't always serious. He also had a sense of humor and wrote humorous letters to friends.

Tesla knew AC systems could send electricity more efficiently and farther than DC systems. The science behind AC power showed it was a better option than DC power lines. But until he could convince people to use AC, he continued to work hard with little recognition.

GAINING GROUND

Tesla kept working on AC power. He did many experiments related to light bulbs. He wanted to make new kinds of lighting and develop a full AC system. In the late 1880s, he finally found people to support him. Some businessmen decided to give him a chance. They backed his research and helped pay for it.

In 1887, Tesla started a new company. It was located in New York City. With Tesla Electric Company, he was finally able to create a full AC system. It included a generator, motor, and transformer. The generator turned a machine's motion into electricity. The motor used the electricity to spin the machine. The transformer then sent the electricity to power other objects, such as light bulbs.

Tesla devoted himself to his inventions, including his
AC motors.

A transformer helps change the voltage of electricity. Voltage is the force that pushes electricity through something such as a wire. Transformers could raise the voltage so electricity could travel long distances without losing much power. This made transformers valuable in AC systems.

TESLA'S X-RAY DISCOVERIES LOST

Tesla experimented with X-rays in the early 1890s. He photographed the bones in his hand with early X-ray technology that he invented. But his work didn't get much credit and wasn't widespread. Years later, his notes were lost. His lab burned down. Without notes, no one could prove exactly what Tesla did. Inventor Wilhelm Röntgen is now known for discovering X-rays in 1895.

STEPS TO GET A PATENT

People go through several steps to get a patent from the government. To do so, they must:

- ANSWER QUESTIONS ABOUT WHAT THE INVENTION IS TO FIND OUT IF IT CAN BE PATENTED.

- CHECK THAT THE IDEA HASN'T BEEN INVENTED ALREADY.

- CHOOSE THE RIGHT TYPE OF PATENT (THERE ARE DIFFERENT KINDS).

- APPLY FOR A PATENT AND WAIT FOR SOMEONE TO REVIEW THE PAPERWORK.

- GET THE APPROVED PATENT IN THE MAIL.

After making the whole AC system, Tesla got seven **patents** for various parts of the system. A patent is proof of someone's idea. It protects an inventor's idea from being stolen by other people who might try to pass the idea off as their own. Tesla's many patents showed his talent as an inventor. From 1888 to 1891, Tesla got 36 patents for his inventions.

CHAPTER FOUR

PARTNERSHIPS AND INVENTIONS

In 1888, Tesla was invited to speak at an event for the American Institute of Electrical Engineers. He discussed AC power. Tesla's talk got the attention of George Westinghouse. Westinghouse was a businessman. He had money to fund Tesla's research. Their meeting led to a successful partnership.

However, Tesla had to make **sacrifices** for funding. In 1888, he sold some of his patents to Westinghouse. If other people wanted to use Tesla's patents to make products, they had to pay to use the ideas. The sale of his patents meant that Westinghouse got the money instead of Tesla. At first, Tesla was paid for each motor that Westinghouse made. But changes in the industry soon put an end to that.

An illustration from the late 1800s shows Tesla giving a presentation about AC power.

George Westinghouse was an inventor as well as a businessman. He got more than 100 patents for his work.

Other power companies were combining into larger companies. Westinghouse's company needed help from new partners to compete with the larger companies. These partners demanded that the original agreement with Tesla be canceled. Tesla would no longer be paid for the motors. Westinghouse reluctantly asked Tesla to end their agreement. Because Westinghouse had always been honest with Tesla, Tesla tore up the contract.

WAR OF THE CURRENTS

Tesla lost a big source of income when the agreement with Westinghouse was canceled. But with the help of Westinghouse, the AC system attracted interest. People wondered if it was a better option than DC power. Westinghouse and Tesla became direct competitors with Edison.

Tesla traveled back to Europe in 1892 to give speeches about AC power. He spoke in London, England, and Paris. He had planned to go to other cities that year, but his mother became ill.

Tesla canceled his plans and went to visit his mother. She was one of the most important people in his life. He stayed with her until her death a few weeks later. Then Tesla returned to the United States.

Chicago, Illinois, was scheduled to host a world's fair in 1893. It would be the first world's fair powered by electricity. People from around the world would attend. Edison and Westinghouse both tried to win the bid to provide the electricity. Westinghouse offered to provide electricity for a lower price than Edison. It was a chance to show how AC power could be useful and cheap. Westinghouse won the deal. Tesla's form of electricity lit the Chicago World's Fair.

The Chicago deal boosted Westinghouse's and Tesla's **reputation**. It helped Westinghouse win another deal, this time to create electricity from Niagara Falls. These large waterfalls lie along the U.S.-Canada border in New York State.

FACT

The 2006 movie *The Prestige* is about magicians from the late 1800s. In it, one magician visits Tesla at his laboratory.

The Electricity Building at the Chicago World's Fair was lit by AC power. Tesla's AC generator was on display in the building.

The first modern power station at Niagara Falls used Westinghouse's AC generators. The station used hydroelectric power to create electricity. Rushing water spun the blades in a **turbine**. The generators turned that energy into electricity. Electricity was sent out from the station using AC systems.

ELECTRIC
SPARK

ELECTRODE

SECONDARY
COIL

PRIMARY
COIL

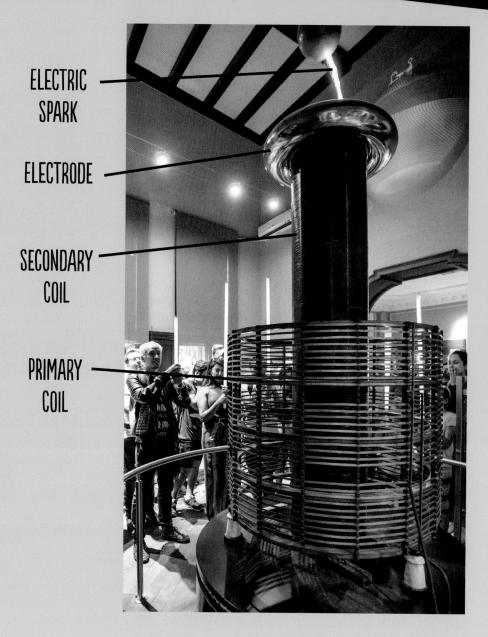

Many people had tried and failed to find a way to harness the falls' energy. In 1896, Westinghouse's Niagara power station supplied power for the city of Buffalo, New York, which was 22 miles (35 kilometers) away. This achievement completed AC power's victory over DC power.

MORE INVENTIONS AND EXPERIMENTS

One of Tesla's most famous inventions was the Tesla coil. He invented it in 1891. The coil let electricity travel through the air as sparks and lightning. It didn't need wires. Electricity traveled through the primary coil first. Then it traveled to the secondary coil, where it increased in voltage. From there, it reached the electrode, where electricity sparked into the air.

The pair of coils acted as a transformer. Transformers are used in many machines. The Tesla coil could generate high-voltage electricity. Other inventions, such as television sets and wireless radio, were made possible by this technology.

Tesla would demonstrate experiments with electricity for visitors in his lab.

Tesla did more speaking events in the United States and other countries. Tesla often let people come to his laboratory. He showed them how his inventions worked.

At his lab, Tesla lit lamps by letting electricity flow over the surface of his body. He did this to prove Edison wrong. Edison had been telling people AC currents were too dangerous.

In 1895, Tesla's New York laboratory burned. The fire started in the basement and ground floors that were not part of his lab. It spread through the whole building and destroyed years of Tesla's notes and equipment. But the disaster didn't stop Tesla's creativity.

Tesla experimented with radio technology. In 1898, he made a small boat that could be moved by remote control. The remote control used radio waves. People didn't believe his invention actually worked. Tesla set up an event at Madison Square Garden in New York City. He directed the boat around a pool with the remote control. He proved his invention worked. Soon, he would take this work across the country.

ECCENTRIC MAN, LASTING LEGACY

In 1899, Tesla moved to Colorado Springs, Colorado. There, he created human-made lightning from his Tesla coil. The massive flashes measured 135 feet (41 meters). He discovered the ground can conduct electricity. That means electric charges can pass through it. Tesla also experimented with wireless power. He surrounded a large field of light bulbs with a wire. The bulbs were not attached to the wire, but when he sent electricity through it, the bulbs lit up.

Additionally, Tesla found the ground can resonate at a certain **frequency**. Resonating means vibrating. Vibrations pass energy through the air or ground in waves.

Tesla continued experimenting with electricity at his lab in Colorado Springs.

Tesla drew up plans for the Tesla Tower, which he imagined would send wireless transmissions. But the tower was never completed.

Tesla's discovery that the ground can resonate was known as electrical resonance. It would play an important role in Tesla's next major project. With electrical resonance, Tesla dreamed of creating a worldwide wireless network. This thought was far ahead of his time. He planned to build a tower that would send signals through the ground. Since the ground was a conductor, the signals could be sent around the world.

Then in 1900, Tesla moved back to New York. J.P. Morgan agreed to fund Tesla's work. Morgan was a powerful banker. Tesla told Morgan of his plans. The network would power telephones, radios, and other systems. Some compare it to an early version of Wi-Fi.

HOW DOES WI-FI WORK?

Tesla's plan for a wireless network was ahead of his time. Today, people use wireless networks every day. The network is known as Wi-Fi. It works because of radio waves sent through the air.

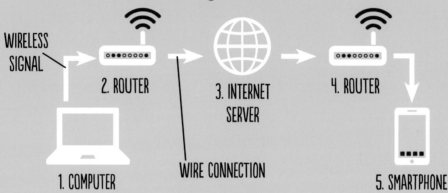

1. A computer codes a message. It sends the message out in a radio signal.

2. A router picks up the signal. It sends the signal through a wire to the internet.

3. The signal is stored on an internet server.

4. Routers in other locations allow other devices to access information on the internet.

5. There are many devices, such as smartphones, that connect to routers through Wi-Fi to receive information.

Tesla started working on a central tower for the network at Long Island, New York. He hoped the communications network would have multiple purposes. He believed it could send messages, weather warnings, business reports, and more. Such technology was hard for most people at the time to imagine. However, Tesla ran out of funds before he could complete the project. Morgan became unhappy with Tesla's grand plan. He worried the network was too huge and unrealistic. He stopped paying for Tesla's work on it.

DEATH AND LEGACY

Tesla's ideas were a major part of many great inventions during his lifetime. Unfortunately, he got neither money nor recognition for most of them. His improvement of DC dynamos benefited Edison— not him. Similarly, his inventions related to the development of radio were not recognized. In 1901, Italian inventor Guglielmo Marconi completed the first radio transmission across the Atlantic Ocean.

The technology Marconi used was based on Tesla's inventions. Tesla had patents for his work. But in 1904, the U.S. Patent Office reversed Tesla's radio patent. It gave credit to Marconi. Marconi became known as the Father of Radio. Tesla was upset. He believed he was the rightful inventor. Tesla spent many years fighting the patent office's decision.

Tesla worked on inventions his whole life. Sometimes he slept as little as two hours a night. He lived alone in a hotel in New York. He had little money. An **eccentric** personality often cast Tesla as an outsider. Sometimes he talked about far-fetched ideas. For example, Tesla claimed that he had invented a death ray that could destroy 10,000 airplanes from 250 miles (400 km) away. There was never any evidence that he had invented such a device.

Even though Tesla worked in scientific fields, he was often excluded from scientific social groups. Some scientists were slow to accept his ideas. They didn't know if they could believe him. Instead, Tesla found friends in the literary and artistic fields.

Tesla continued to work on inventions throughout his life.

Tesla also had some behaviors that others thought were unusual. He was obsessed with the numeral 3. Tesla had **compulsive** washing habits. He believed he needed to wash even when he was already clean. Historians later realized these were signs of a mental illness. Tesla may have had obsessive-compulsive disorder. People with this illness can't control some of their thoughts and actions.

Over time, Tesla's health declined. His body and mind grew unwell. He died January 7, 1943, at age 87.

FINALLY RECOGNIZED

Following Tesla's death, the U.S. Supreme Court acknowledged his work with radio. It **voided** four of Marconi's patents and put them in Tesla's name. Its decisions showed Tesla was responsible for some radio inventions. As years went on, historians realized Tesla's impact on science. They looked into all his known experiments and work. But they still haven't discovered everything Tesla did.

TESLA THE AUTHOR

Tesla wrote several books. Some were about his life. Others focused on and explained his research or inventions. He wrote *A Means for Furthering Peace* in 1905. It was about the problems of war, and it explored ideas about how humans could learn to live in peace. He also wrote an autobiography titled *My Inventions* in 1919.

Some historians guess Tesla created more than 300 inventions. But they aren't exactly sure because some of his inventions were not patented. Also many of his inventions were closely related to each other. So it is possible that many of his ideas were unpatented. Tesla's work continues to change people's lives. Since his death, at least three Nobel Prize winners have mentioned Tesla's name. They have honored Tesla for paving the way for their achievements.

Tesla's legacy lives on. He is remembered as a brilliant and hardworking engineer. His ideas about wireless communication were ahead of his time. He's best known for inventing the first AC motor and improving AC technology. Tesla's AC system is a global standard for power systems today.

TIMELINE

1856: Nikola Tesla is born in Smiljan, Croatia, on July 10.

1882: Tesla comes up with an idea for rotating magnetic fields and moves to Paris, France.

1884: Tesla moves to the United States and works at Thomas Edison's headquarters in New York City.

1893: Tesla's AC power lights the Chicago World's Fair.

1895: Tesla's New York laboratory burns down, destroying years of work.

1898: Tesla drives a radio-controlled boat around a pool in Madison Square Garden.

1899: Tesla moves to Colorado Springs, Colorado.

1900: Tesla moves back to New York, where he lives and works until his death.

1904: The U.S. patent office reverses Tesla's radio patent and gives it to Guglielmo Marconi.

1943: Tesla dies on January 7.

compulsive (kuhm-PUHL-siv)
having strong urges to do something even when it does not need to be done

eccentric (eks-EN-trik)
having unusual behavior

engineer (en-juh-NEER)
a person who invents, improves, designs, and works with devices

frequency (FREE-kwuhn-see)
the number of times something happens over a certain period of time

patents (PA-tents)
papers that prove someone's idea or invention

reputation (rep-yoo-TAY-shuhn)
the behavior or actions someone is known for

turbine (TUR-bine)
a machine with a wheel or rotor that turns with the flow of something such as water or wind

virtual reality (VER-choo-uhl re-A-lih-tee)
technology that displays an environment that people can experience with multiple senses but isn't physically present

voided (VOY-did)
canceled

READ MORE

Gigliotti, Jim. *Who Was Nikola Tesla?* New York: Penguin Random House, 2018.

Klepeis, Alicia Z. *The Future of Transportation: From Electric Cars to Jet Packs.* North Mankato, MN: Capstone Press, 2020.

Sobey, Ed. *Electrical Engineering: Learn It, Try It!* North Mankato, MN: Capstone Press, 2018.

INTERNET SITES

The Nobel Prize: Nobel Prize Facts
https://www.nobelprize.org/prizes/facts/nobel-prize-facts/

Tesla Universe: Nikola Tesla Timeline
https://teslauniverse.com/nikola-tesla/timeline/1856-birth-nikola-tesla

U.S. Department of Energy: The War of the Currents: AC vs. DC Power
https://www.energy.gov/articles/war-currents-ac-vs-dc-power

alternating current (AC), 8-9, 11, 14, 17, 18, 20, 22-23, 24, 27-29, 31, 33, 43
Austria, 8

Batchelor, Charles, 15

Chicago, Illinois, 28
Colorado, 6, 34
Croatia, 6
Czech Republic, 9

direct current (DC), 8-9, 12, 14, 17, 20, 27, 31, 39

Edison, Thomas, 12, 14-15, 17, 18, 27-28, 33, 39, 43
England, 27

Hungary, 11

magnetic fields, 4, 11
Marconi, Guglielmo, 39-40, 42
Morgan, J.P., 37, 39

New York City, 14-15, 20, 33

Paris, France, 12, 15, 27
patents, 23, 24, 40, 42-43

radio, 32-33, 37, 38, 39-40, 42

Serbia, 6

Tesla coil, 30, 31, 34

virtual reality, 6

Westinghouse, George, 24, 27-29

X-rays, 22